KT-244-746

THE TERRIBLE TWOS

Compiled by

SARAH KENNEDY

BBC BOOKS

This book is published to accompany
BBC Children in Need
televised and broadcast in November, 1994.

Published by BBC Books,
a division of BBC Enterprises Limited,
Woodlands, 80 Wood Lane,
London W12 0TT.

First published 1994
Reprinted 1994

ISBN 0 563 37114 5

Printed and bound in Great Britain by Butler and Tanner Ltd, Frome

Set in Palatino

Printed paper case printed by Lawrence Allen Ltd, Weston-super-Mare

A royalty of 10% of the retail price of this book will be paid to
BBC CHILDREN IN NEED
on every copy sold.

Sarah Kennedy and BBC Books have made every effort to contact the contributors to this book. Should they have failed to do so, they will be pleased to correct this, after notification, at the earliest possible opportunity.

Preface

'I'm Molly Alice Hughes and I'm two-and-a-half, Sarah Kennedy.'

Molly, the younger of the two cover girls, is to blame for *The Terrible Twos*. On asked what she wanted for lunch, she replied with the confidence of Julius Caesar, 'Taramasalata, Mummy'.

By sheer coincidence, a week later I was listening to Jimmy Young talking to his food expert Toni De Angeli:

T De A: 'Taramasalata is good value this weekend, Jim.'

JY: (*Genuinely perplexed*) 'What's taramasalata?'

T De A: 'Er ... well ... a rather elaborate fish paste, Jim ...'

Jim, age and experience, out-manoeuvred by a two-and-a-half year old.

Your letters reflect how youngsters out-wit us on various subjects. Do we adults stone-clad ourselves from life — sex, religion, relationships, money, lavatories, basic truths? The young ones, oblivious, cut through the rubbish and cant.

Read on, you'll have a good chuckle — and thank you so much for the pleasure you have given me and all Radio Two's Dawn Patrol listeners. And thank you, too, for the contribution you've made to BBC Children in Need by buying a copy of *The Terrible Twos*. A personal 'thank you' should go to Barbara Nash, without whose gentle guidance we wouldn't have a book at all.

I am delighted to say that a BBC Radio Collection cassette entitled *The Terrible Twos* and featuring many other letters, is also available.

Now let's read on — two of my personal favourites:

'One day while out walking with my two sons, someone came up to me and asked the way to the mill. I gave directions and the person thanked

me. As he turned to walk off, one of my sons said: "I don't think people should go out if they don't know where they are going"'!

And:

'Our daughter, Susan, was about three (she's now in her thirties) and we were on a crowded bus. The conductor was a large black gentleman and Susan, after staring at him for a long time, suddenly said in a very loud voice, "Daddy, why are we white?"'

And, finally, Sarah Kennedy — yes, me — aged two-and-a-half, learning to read:

SK's Dad: (*Spelling out each syllable)* 'C ... A ... T ... spells cat, Sarah. S ... A ... T ... spells sat, Sarah. Now, your turn, Sarah ... M ... A ... T ... spells ... ?'

SK: (*Completely bewildered by previous examples, but desperate to come up with something, looks round for inspiration, and delivers*) 'Yellow.'

Father retreats to the pub.

How I got into the BBC, God alone knows!

Molly said she'd do the front cover picture for this book if she got a Pudsey Bear, a hamburger and could then go swimming with Sarah Kennedy. She'll be head of MI5-and-a-half soon!

Sarah Kennedy

Embarrassment

Doing my first teaching practice back in the mid-thirties at a school called People's College, I set a composition exercise called 'Wintertime'. When marking the exercise, I came upon a 'beaut', and I quote:

'I don't like winter mornings and going to school in the cold, so that's why I get into bed with Mum and the lodger before I get up.'

Spider Davis

Granddaughter Louise was in a real 'paddy' and wouldn't sit at the dinner table to eat.

Andy, her dad, lost his patience and told her he had thrown her dinner in the bin. '

Get me my f...ing knife,' Louise screamed at the top of her voice.

Andy stopped dead in his tracks, wondering where she had heard such filthy language and how to deal with it. Then the penny suddenly dropped as he realized she was saying fork and knife.

We are now trying to get her to say knife and fork!

Jill Cattle

Once on a coach trip, when my son was nearly five and very small for his age, I sat him on my knee.

Out of the blue, he announced loudly, 'If the man asks me how old I am, shall I say three?'

I shrivelled in my seat!

Mrs G.A. Collins

While being assessed for school, my grandson, was asked:

'What is a bush?'

After a moment or two, he said:

'They have them in the park, and you go wee-wees behind them.'

Mrs V. M. Hallett

THE TERRIBLE TWOS

When my daughter, Elisa, was small, my friend, Maureen, was on her annual visit and, as a treat, we'd arranged to go out together to see a show and have a meal beforehand leaving Daddy to babysit.

Elisa was about five or six and very 'into' Barbie dolls with their ballgowns all glittering with sequins, etc.

She watched 'Auntie' Maureen getting ready in her smart wool dress, and said perplexed, 'Auntie Maureen, did you know Mummy and you were going out tonight?'

'Oh, yes, love,' said Maureen, 'Mummy booked tickets for the show in advance.'

'Oh,' said Elisa sadly, 'then it's such a pity you didn't bring something decent to wear.'

Valerie King

An insurance collector had been calling at my home every week for years, so he was more like a friend. But I had never before had to tell him I couldn't pay him.

Consequently, one week when I really was short of money, I was feeling extremely awkward at having to ask him if I could leave it till next week. Then, when he knocked on the door, I suddenly had a brainwave and ushered myself and my two little girls into the kitchen at the back of the house, shushing them and trying to make it look as if we were playing hide-and-seek. Eventually, after knocking three times, he went away.

The following week when he called, I opened the door to him with a cheery grin and a jolly 'Hallo'.

'Hallo,' he answered, 'I called last week, but you weren't in.'

Before I could reply, my daughter, aged four, chipped in, 'Yes, we were. We were hiding from you in the kitchen'.

Margaret Lakeman

THE TERRIBLE TWOS

A particular fault of my son's early letters was a tendency to miss out consonants, especially at the end of words such as 'they', pronouncing it without a 'y' or 'your' without an 'r'.

His Aunts in the country, who kept a farm, were not therefore over-impressed with a thank-you letter that commenced with the solicitous enquiry, 'I hope you cows are all right'.

Tony Dudmesh

A teacher set her class an essay on the subject of 'Washday Monday'.

One child wrote: 'On Washday Monday my Mother gets up early and looks out of the window. If it's a nice day she goes downstairs and gets on with the washing. If it's raining, she says, "Bugger it," and goes back to bed.'

Connie MacKinnon

THE TERRIBLE TWOS

When my middle son, Adam, was six I was expecting our third child and his headmaster's mother said, 'I hear Mummy is going to have another baby — would you like a brother or sister?'

Adam: 'A brother.'

Mrs S: 'And what about Mummy? What would she like?'

Adam: 'A girl.'

Mrs S: 'And what about Daddy? What would he like?'

Adam: 'Oh, he doesn't want a baby at all.'

Liz Bidwell

A woman and her four-year-old daughter were in a shop buying a few groceries, and chatting to the shopkeeper, a somewhat elderly gentleman. They were discussing at some length the forthcoming marriage of one of the village girls.

Towards the end of the conversation, the shopkeeper leaned over the counter and spoke to the child.

'What about you? Are you going to get married when you grow up, Anne?' he asked.

'Yes,' replied Anne.

'Are you going to marry me?' asked the shopkeeper.

'No!' replied Anne.

'Why not?'

'Because,' said Anne, 'my Mummy says you're a dirty old man.'

Tom Reynolds

At my younger son's Christening, Graham, then aged 'two-and-a-lot' (two-and-three-quarters actually), was feeling left out.

At the party afterwards he sidled up to an elderly maiden aunt and confided in a wonderful stage whisper, 'I've got new pants on and they're grown-up ones. They've got a hole to wee through, would you like to see?'

Julie Grey

THE TERRIBLE TWOS

Mavis had told her three-year-old daughter, Fiona, to be on her best behaviour when she visited one of her aunts who was a stickler for good manners.

'Always say "please" and "thank you,"' cautioned Mavis, 'and, whatever you do, always be polite.'

At lunch, the aunt enquired of Fiona:

'Can you manage the meat, or would you like me to help and cut it up for you?'

'No, thank you,' Fiona replied, 'I can manage on my own. We sometimes have meat as tough as this at home.'

Roger Wilson

Near-friends of mine were having an extension built to their home and their three-year-old, Julia, was closely involved 'helping' the builders with her bucket and spade.

On Friday the foreman arrived with the workmen's wage-packets and Julia was mortified to find she had not been included, running into her mother, with bottom lip a-quiver.

The following week the men got together, putting money in themselves, and organized a wage-packet for her, with her name on and complete with tax and national insurance contributions.

This time Julia was overjoyed — her very own wages — and she immediately demanded to be taken to the sweet shop to spend the money.

Despite the shop being crowded, the shopkeeper joined in the fun putting the change back in the wage-packet, and, as they were leaving, he asked:

'Will you be working again next week, Julia?'

'I'm not sure,' she replied in that piercing voice only children have. 'It depends if they deliver the f...ing bricks.'

Jan Owens

THE TERRIBLE TWOS

Eddie and I were married in 1946 and I gave birth to our second son, Steven, on our sixth wedding anniversary.

On his first day at school, Steven proudly announced to the class:

'I was born on Mummy's wedding day.'

Maude Milliss

My granddaughter, Sarah, then aged three years, was walking along the High Street with her parents. In front of them, a large Boxer dog was being taken for a walk by the owner.

My daughter couldn't understand why the child kept bending down, peering at the dog's hind quarters.

On being told to walk properly, she said in a loud clear voice, 'Doesn't that dog look like Daddy'.

Margaret Hillier

We spent last year at a very up-market hotel in Scotland, with our two young sons, aged three and five.

One morning at breakfast, my husband and the boys finished and left the dining-room before I did.

Ten minutes later the children reappeared, threading their way through tables of people sedately murmuring over their croissants.

When they were about twenty feet away from me, I asked, 'Where's Daddy?'

In bell-like tones the three-year-old replied, 'He's having a poo!'

I lost consciousness at this point.

Kim Shore

My wife was a non-drinker and non-smoker but, during the Christmas festivities at a friend's party, she made an exception to the rule and drank quite a few 'shorts', etc.

Three-year-old Astrid, tired of playing, went to sit on her mother's lap, but, once there, complained, 'Phew, Mummy, you smell of Daddy.'

Tony Bowler

THE TERRIBLE TWOS

We were at a family cocktail party, and one of the family guests was Uncle Arthur who had something of a reputation for being a rather heavy drinker.

The couple giving the party had a small daughter, aged about four, and, as a special treat, she was allowed to hand round the cocktail snacks.

After her Uncle Arthur had taken a handful of cheese-straws, the small child, being particularly perceptive, returned to her mother and announced in a voice that all could hear (as only a small child can do), 'Mummy, Uncle Arthur doesn't drink like a fish. He drinks like any one else.'

Chris Short

THE TERRIBLE TWOS

I had arranged to collect a neighbour's children, along with my own, when nursery school closed. As the children piled into the back of the car, one little girl said, 'Oh, Mrs Fey, your hair looks really lovely today'.

Before I could say a thing, my dear son leaned over the front seat where I was sitting, ready to drive off, and putting thumb and forefinger together, he yanked at the crown of my head, shouting gleefully, 'It's a wig'.

You can imagine my embarrassment as I sat there with my own hair plastered closely to my head, while the wig flew through the air!

Valerie Fey

My granddaughter was getting her three children ready for school when Ben, aged four-and-a-half, started to cry, saying he didn't want to go.

After several minutes of coaxing, his Mam ended with, 'You like school, Ben, you know you do'.

'I know,' Ben answered, 'but it's that little girl with long plaits. She keeps loving me all the time.'

Vida Saunders

THE TERRIBLE TWOS

When my son (now thirty) was little, we travelled by bus regularly.

One day my husband came with us and a *very* beautiful woman got on.

'Isn't she attractive,' my hubby said.

A couple of days later, Son and I were on the bus when the woman got on again, and in *that* voice that every mother dreads, he said, 'Oh, look, Mum, it's that lady Daddy says is a TRACTOR.'

Kath

Our friend, Maxine, takes a ballet class of three year olds, and as the occasional accident happens, Maxine keeps a spare pair of pants at the ready.

Well, 'It' happened, and the spare pair was duly lent, with instructions to bring them back next lesson.

The next week a room full of Mums and Dads were dropping off their little darlings, when this one's little darling piped up in a loud voice, 'Daddy's brought your knickers back'.

Red-faced Maxine!

Kathleen Lawton

Logic

My son and daughter-in-law are trying hard to bring up their family in a peaceful manner — it is not easy. They regularly tell the children 'We fight with words not deeds'.

One day my grandson came home from his playgroup very indignant because one of the other children had hit him.

His Mummy sympathized with him, but said, 'I hope you told him we fight with words not deeds'.

Very earnestly, my grandson replied, 'Yes, I did, Mummy ... then I hit him.'

Ann Hayden

When my grandson, John, was seven, I gave him a diary. He filled in his name, address and phone number in the spaces provided, then, coming to 'Blood Group', asked me what his was.

I replied that I didn't know, but if he ever went to a hospital some one would use a needle to take a sample of his blood, and would certainly tell him.

Before I could say more, he interrupted me, saying, 'I'm not going to bother with any of that. I shall just put down Red'.

Margaret Gaukroger

David, then only five, was with the family having lunch at a pub. His Mother and I were discussing his teacher who, unfortunately, had just had a miscarriage.

David, listening to the pair of us talking, said, 'What's a miscarriage, Mum?'

Red-faced, his mother said in a low voice, 'It's when you lose a baby. Now eat your chips.'

He ate a chip with a thoughtful look on his face, then suddenly said in a loud voice, 'My dad must have had a miscarriage when he lost me in Bolton'.

Chris and Avis Parr

THE TERRIBLE TWOS

My granddaughter, Victoria, is two-and-three-quarters years old. Last Monday, she had her first ballet lesson. There are ten children in the class, all looking very pretty in their little leotards.

Teacher asked the children to pretend to hold up an open umbrella and dance around to music.

Victoria never moved and when asked by teacher why she didn't take part she said, 'I don't need an umbrella — I pulled up my hood'.

Mrs S. Price

THE TERRIBLE TWOS

One Sunday I was washing my car when a squeaky little voice piped up, 'Excuse me ...'

I turned round and saw a young boy all of five years of age.

'Hallo,' I said. 'What can I do for you?'

'What's your name?' he replied.

'Stanley.' I answered. 'What's yours?'

'Jerry,' he said.

'That's a nice name,' I said, and carried on cleaning the car.

'Excuse me,' the squeaky voice piped up again, and, when I turned and faced him, he said, 'Can I be your mate?'

I said that I thought I might be a little old for him, and suggested he make friends with someone his own age.

He was somewhat crestfallen by this, and said, 'I have only just moved in and I don't know any one'.

I pondered, then said, 'I tell you what — until you find someone your own age — I'll be your mate.'

He thanked me and meandered off, and I thought that was that. How wrong one can be. Every Sunday morning the front-door bell would ring and, when my wife answered it, there would be Jerry saying: 'Is Stan coming out?'

So, whatever I was doing, I would take time out and go into the garden with him and have a chat. This went on for quite a while until, one Sunday morning, my wife once again opened the door, and there was Jerry with his usual, 'Is Stan coming out?'

On this occasion when my wife replied I was busy, he was crestfallen and said, 'What's he doing?'

My wife explained that I was decorating.

'Decorating,' he said absolutely aghast, 'decorating! We don't decorate — we move.'

The following Sunday, he thanked me for being his friend, then informed me he had found someone his own age and wouldn't be calling again.

Stan Budd

THE TERRIBLE TWOS

Our great aunt came to stay and, while she was with us, our dear grandmother (who lived next door) passed away. Needless to say, there was much activity first thing in the morning — with people coming and going next door.

My young brother, five years old, realized something special was afoot and, in great excitement, dashed upstairs to my great aunt who was still in bed and said: 'Come on, Auntie, quick, wake up, Nanna's dead, and it's your turn next'.

Patricia Levett

My grandson, Matthew, had been having trouble controlling his bowels, and my daughter had taken him to the doctor. When things cleared up, the doctor told her to stop the medication.

Over Christmas, he had an accident and my daughter told him off. He replied that she hadn't given him his medicine. When she told him the doctor said he didn't need it, he replied, 'Doctors don't know everything'.

There's no answer to that, is there?

Ruth Wilkes

My son, Gareth (I'm very proud to say) is a Welsh Rugby Union Referee. When he first started to referee some of the more important games, some of them were televised.

I was sitting with my grandson, Aled, watching Gareth and, afterwards, I said, 'Wasn't it exciting watching Daddy on Television. What did you think of it?'

'Oh, it was all right,' he replied, 'but I wish he would play nicely with the others instead of blowing that whistle and putting his hand in the air.'

Joan Simmonds

My grandson was asking his Mother what time of day he was born.

'One o'clock in the morning,' she told him.

'I hope I didn't wake you up,' he said.

D. Dunston

THE TERRIBLE TWOS

Gareth had been to London for the day, and his mother had bought him a toy policeman's helmet. He wore it very proudly on the train journey returning to Guildford. The carriage was packed with city commuters.

Gareth sat quietly for a long time, and then suddenly turned and addressed the bowler-hatted gent next to him, saying, 'I'm not really a policeman you know — underneath this helmet I'm just an ordinary person.'

Roy Cole

THE TERRIBLE TWOS

While working as a midwife I delivered a baby in the morning at the mother's home and returned later for the evening visit.

I was greeted at the door by the two-year-old who said:

'Have you come to take it back again? We've had it all day.'

Marjorie Davies

My daughter had a doctor's appointment for a blood-pressure check, so asked little Louise to hurry up.

'We are going to the doctor' she explained.

'Why?' Louise replied. 'Don't I feel very well?'

Joan Langridge

Each child was asked to learn a verse and recite it to proud mums.

When it was Steven's turn, he stood up, and in a well-rehearsed country-bumpkin accent, said:

'Little birdie in the sky, did a packet in my eye,
damn good job pigs can't fly.'

My husband had been busy wickedly rehearsing him behind my back.

Mary Bachini

My daughter was just home with her new baby son, and the district nurse called.

The nurse looked at the baby and said, 'Isn't he like his Daddy'.

'No he's not,' said Matthew aged four, 'he hasn't got a moustache.'

Janet McCumiskey

I told John we were going shopping with a friend.

'Oh, no,' he said, 'not that Marks-Expensive shop — you always spend so long there.'

Diane Miller

THE TERRIBLE TWOS

One Sunday when my daughter, Monique, was coming up to four, we drove down to Littlehampton.

After forty-five miles of her repeatedly asking, 'Are we there yet?', I pointed to a huge blue sign board and read out loud, 'Welcome to Littlehampton'.

There was a short pause.

'Did that sign really say that, Daddy?'

'Yes,' I said. 'Why?'

'How did they know we were coming?' she replied mystified.

Clive Kavanagh

A little boy was sitting in a cardboard box pretending to drive madly, and accompanying himself with car-tyre screams as he belted across the room.

'You in your motor car, then?' asked my friend to the little one.

'No,' he said, staring at her as if she was mad, 'I'm in a Box.'

Val O'Grady

Some years ago, my small daughter (four-and-a-half years) had her first PE lesson at her new 'big' school.

She said she had enjoyed it and added reassuringly, 'It's all right, Mummy, I didn't let the boys see my knickers.'

'How did you manage that?' I replied.

'Well,' she answered. 'I took them off!'

Julia Marshall

As a would-be fattie constantly fighting the battle of the bulge my Mother always took artificial sweeteners in tea and coffee.

While entertaining friends for coffee one morning, she produced the sugar bowl which was duly passed round.

My little brother looked on in fascination as various people helped themselves and then proclaimed, 'My Mum doesn't have sugar in her coffee — she has aspirins.'!

Caroline Cassells

THE TERRIBLE TWOS

Roanne and Steven are my step-grandchildren. They were visiting, and the three of us were sitting in the garden. The conversation went like this:

Roanne: 'Barbara, why have you got a dish of dog food in the garden under the trees?'

Me: 'It's there for my hedgehog. He likes dog food.'

Roanne: 'If we are very quiet, might we see him?'

Me: 'I don't think so, dear. He sleeps during the day and only wakes up at night.'

Knowing how progressive their parents are in their teachings, I thought they might know the word 'nocturnal', so I added, 'Do you know what we call someone who does that?'

Roanne: 'No, I don't.'

Steven: 'I do, Barbara. They are called burglars.'

Barbara Godfrey

THE TERRIBLE TWOS

Our son, who could swim, was playing in the pool with a polystyrene float. At one point, he slipped from this into the water which was very cold.

This caused Ian, an asthmatic, to lose his breath, and being then unable to shout, he was going under for the third time when he was spotted simultaneously by the lifeguard and a friend who both dived into the pool to his rescue.

The lifeguard took Ian to the shower-room to get him warmed up.

Ian, no worse for his experience, was chatting away with him.

The lifeguard explained that he would normally provide people like Ian with a drink, but went on to say that because it was so early in the season he had no stock of drinks, so would Ian like a glass of water instead.

'Don't you think I've had enough water already,' Ian replied.

Win and Neil Morley

My daughters, Sarah and Catherine, are now aged nineteen and twenty-one. When Sarah was five years old she attended ballet classes held in a hall on convent land. One evening, Catherine, then aged three years old, came with me to collect Sarah after her lesson.

We were waiting in the car and, on this particular evening, there were a number of Sisters walking around the grounds. Taken by their attire, Catherine wanted to know who these ladies were.

I explained very carefully that they were called Sisters or nuns, and that they had given up all their belongings, jewellery, clothes, everything, to live in the convent and work for God.

Catherine thought for a while and then said, 'Is that why they are called Nuns, 'cause they haven't got none'?

Janice Rolls

THE TERRIBLE TWOS

Picture the scene ... a very hot summer's day, a visitation to our street by the Water Board. The street was looking like a weird moon-scape with its array of deep craters, as the workmen replaced our ageing main's supply.

My youngest daughter Amy (aged about nine at the time) came skipping up the street, clutching a bottle of pop. She stopped at the crater outside our house, and peered down into the hole at the workman below ground level.

'Would you like a cup of tea?' she asked.

The workman looked up hopefully, leaning on his shovel, as he wiped the sweat from his brow. With a great sigh, he replied, 'Aw, I'd *luv* a cup!'

'Tough!' my daughter replied with a really impish smile. 'The water's off!'

Roy Garner

THE TERRIBLE TWOS

David was at school and learning to read. He was at the stage where he read aloud everything in sight.

We were travelling to Scotland on holiday, and David and his younger sister were sitting in the back of the car. As usual, David was reading aloud the street names, etc., (not getting them all correct, I might add).

After a while, he said, 'Why are so many houses called "Bed and Breakfast?"'

Margaret Slater

A policeman, proceeding in a westerly direction, was passing by residential premises, when he heard the cry:

'Stick 'em up.'

Turning apprehensively, he saw a small figure, not more than five years old, in a three-cornered hat, a blanket for a cloak, a cap-gun in the shape of a flint-lock.

Correcting the young villain, he said:

'If you want to be a true Highwayman, what you have to say is, 'Stand up and deliver — your money or your life.'

The boy's eyes narrowed, and his brow furrowed in thought, as the policeman continued on his beat.

Later that same day, as the policeman was proceeding in an easterly direction, the same cloaked figure leapt out from behind the front gatepost, shouting:

'Stock 'em up. Your money or your liver.'

PC John Gisbey

Two-and-a-half-year-old Grace was quite a character. Taken to a Children's Service, she listened to the Vicar's address patiently for about six minutes, then stood on a pew and said in a loud voice, 'ENOUGH'. (Her new word).

She, like Mrs Thatcher, will go far!

Pamela McCann

THE TERRIBLE TWOS

Our neighbours' little boy, James, aged two-and-a-half, shouted from the kitchen, 'Mum, Mum, there's a rat in here.'

Mum, Caroline, rushed panic-stricken into the kitchen shouting, 'Where, where?'

'There,' said James, pointing.

It was an ANT.

Rosemarie and Harry Rose

When my younger sister and I were about three and four years old, an Auntie came to stay with us from the Isle of Man.

My sister was sat on Auntie's knee, and Dorothy, my sister, started pulling up Auntie's skirts.

Our mother scolded Dorothy and asked what she was doing.

'I am looking for her third leg,' she said.

She thought all Isle of Man people had three legs!

Mildred Holding

My small granddaughter, Chlöe, who lives in Warwickshire, was out with her parents last summer and saw, for the first time, a pond full of goldfish.

'Mummy,' she called excitedly, 'come and see all of these carrots.'

Ann Thorne

Gemma, now eight, was only two-and-a-half at the time of this incident, and was refused something she had requested.

Her quick reply was, 'I *want* what I want, and I want it *now*.'

Coming from such a tiny tot, this was really something. She will go far!

Doreen Ralph

THE TERRIBLE TWOS

Grandma was taking her two grandchildren, Philip and Rosie, on a walk. Philip was walking and Rosie was in the push-chair.
While feeding the ducks on a nearby pond, Philip noticed some horse manure (the area is used to exercise horses). As children do, he proceeded to ask Nanny some very awkward questions about the 'deposit'.

Nanny felt she had successfully navigated the difficulty, but unfortunately ended up by saying, 'And sometimes we collect it and throw it on our roses'.

On turning round she noticed Rosie crying her eyes out in the pushchair.

When asked what was wrong, Rosie said, 'You're not throwing *that* over me!'

Joyce Crowther

My next-door neighbour's friend had a young grandson staying with her over night.

In the morning, she went into his bedroom, wearing a pretty pink négligé.

Child: 'Grandma, you look just like Madame Butterfly.'

Grandma (preening): 'Thank you, darling, but *how* do you know about her?'

Child: 'It's the name of our school pig.'

Margaret Newton

My grandson, Christopher (then aged three), was having lunch with me near the dining-room window.

Suddenly a bumble-bee hit the window and flew off.

'What was that I nearly saw?' Christopher said, looking round.

Pauline Nicholson

THE TERRIBLE TWOS

When my daughter Lindsay was three (now twenty-five) she went into the lounge and put the TV on. I was in the kitchen.
She came running out to me and said, 'Mummy, there were these dogs racing on the TV and a rabbit got in with them, and he shouldn't have been there, and he won!'

Jan Hodgkiss

THE TERRIBLE TWOS

There had been a wax crayon lying on the side of the stairs for a few days, then suddenly there was scribble on the grey gloss paint under it. Idly, I said to Lucy as I took her upstairs, 'I wonder who did that scribble there?' 'I don't know,' Lucy said. 'But if it was me, it wasn't my fault as there wasn't any paper there'.

Sue Wells

My niece's little boy is five. I asked him what he'd like to be when he grew up. He thought for a few minutes and answered, 'A vet, but, before that, I am going to learn to swim so that I can take out the medicine to the fish when they are ill'.

Peggy Kieser

THE TERRIBLE TWOS

Some years ago I was down in Kent visiting my cousin and we went to Canterbury for the day, strolling around the Cathedral with our children soaking in the history.

We suddenly heard a very loud whisper from her son, Colin, who was around eight years old at the time and now twenty-four. Speaking with a pronounced London accent, he said, 'Mum, Mum, come over 'ere and see where Becket 'copt it.'

He was standing at the spot where Thomas à Becket was gruesomely murdered!

Mary Penney

My four-year-old son early one morning:

'Mum, how long is a tube of toothpaste?'

Mum perplexed: 'I don't really know, dear, as long as the tube, I suppose'.

Son: 'No, Mum, it goes all along your bedroom wall, then along the other ones.'

And it did!

Geoff Poole

Four-year-old Vicky (now aged six) was happily playing in the living-room while Mummy was busy in the kitchen.

On coming back into the living-room, Mummy noticed to her horror that her very wide nets had dramatically changed shape — and were now cut like 'Jardinière' in the middle.

On being asked why she had cut them, Vicky replied, 'So that my dollies can see out'.

Mummy, needless to say, was not amused!

Doreen Ralph

THE TERRIBLE TWOS

Years ago, my sister took her small daughter, Anneva, out for a walk. They came across a funeral at the local parish church and questions were asked about the big box being carried into the church.

My sister explained as best she could — ending with the fact that the person was going to heaven to be with Jesus.

Later that day there was a rumble of thunder, and a little voice said, '*That* didn't take long'.

'What didn't take long?', my sister asked puzzled.

'Well, for that man to get to heaven.' Anneva replied. 'I can hear Jesus opening the box.'

Margaret Mann

THE TERRIBLE TWOS

My son, Alan, was taking Thomas, my grandson, and myself to the coast for a day out. On the way, Thomas, in the child-seat at the back of the car, dropped off to sleep.

As we passed a field that was obviously having muck spread, I was prompted to comment to my son that the smell would not only bring tears to your eyes, but would put hairs on your chest.

I glanced behind to see if Thomas was all right. His eyes were closed, but he was grinning from ear to ear, shaking his head slowly from side to side.

'Somebody,' he said, 'has trumped, and it wasn't me.'

Margret Bennett

One day while out walking with my two sons, someone came up to me and asked the way to the mill.

I gave directions and the person thanked me. As he turned to walk off, one of my sons said:

'I don't think people should go out if they don't know where they are going.'

Valerie Hawkins

When my daughter, Catherine, was about four years old, she stood in the bathroom watching me dress and said:

'Mummy, why do you wear *little* knickers and have a big botty, and I wear *big* knickers and have a little botty?'

Well, there was no answer to that then, and, today, when I find myself squeezing into my underwear, I still think of this!

Judi Morgan

THE TERRIBLE TWOS

My daughter, Lucie, was just two when I first brought her brother, Paul, home from hospital.

We had been home for a few days and there had been a stream of friends and relatives to see us. Most of them had been very good about admiring Lucie as well, so that she wouldn't be too jealous, but one couple concentrated all their attention on Paul.

This was too much for Lucie, who stomped out into the garden, and, returning after a few minutes, said:

'Mummy, I've taken my knickers off, put them in a puddle, and stamped on them.'

Bridget Farrer

I was sitting on a train with my young son, Benjamin. A couple of seats in front of us was a teenage Punk Rocker with orange hair, cut in Mohican style, which had been coiffeured vertically one foot above his head.

I could see that Ben was transfixed, and my worst dreads were realized when he said in a loud voice, 'Mummy, why does that man look like a chicken-birdie?'

Mrs L B Brown

I was walking my collie dog, Tam, on the beach when he suddenly ran ahead and lifted his leg in a pool of water near to the breakwater where a little boy was making sandcastles.

'James,' the boy's mother called urgently, 'come here?'

'Why?' James called back.

'Because,' his mother replied, 'that dog has just done a wee-wee.'

'So what,' James replied, 'so have I.'

Jill Thornton

THE TERRIBLE TWOS

This anecdote involves my niece, Aimee, aged two.

It occurred when her Mum and Dad were defrosting the fridge, reaching that part of the process where the defrosted water runs all over the kitchen floor.

Aimee, who had just mastered the art of walking unaided and was enjoying the associated freedom, was pottering around downstairs in her playclothes.

A little while later, Mum and Dad, alerted by the noises and grunts that always accompany tinies who have just learned to manage stairs alone, turned round.

Aimee, having sized up the significance of the occasion stood there, in the kitchen doorway, red-faced from her climbing efforts, and completely naked except for a pair of Wellington boots!

Sylvia Mann

THE TERRIBLE TWOS

A friend of mine, together with her daughter and three-year-old granddaughter, were walking round a well-known DIY store, with the intention of ordering a bathroom suite.

Suddenly her granddaughter had gone missing, and, after a frantic search, they found her, in full view of all the public, sitting on a display toilet with her knickers round her ankles, having a little light relief.

When a harassed male shop assistant explained to her that this toilet was for display purposes only, she said:

'Go away. It's *very* rude to watch ladies on the toilet.'

Jean Denney

Religion

The sideboard was groaning with Easter eggs and presents, so my sister felt that she should tell her children the religious significance of Easter.

After lunch, Susan was wanting to get down from the table.

Mother: 'Say your grace, Susan, then you can leave the table.'

Susan: 'Not much good today — he's dead!'

Collyn Freeland

My grandson, Neil, aged six, exasperated with his sister Jenny, aged four, said: 'You think you know everything, Jenny, don't you?'

Jenny: 'Well, I do, then.'

Neil: 'Well, what is God made of then?'

Jenny: 'God is made of very strong metal.'

Mr J. L. Taylor

My mother died when my daughter, Jenny, was a babe in arms, but she knows her Nanny Rose's house because it has been up for sale for a long time, and she regularly visits it with her Daddy to keep the place maintained and the lawns cut. This is not Jenny's favourite outing because there is not much to amuse a two-year-old in an empty house.

Anyway, through playgroup, Jenny suddenly became aware that she did not have even one Granddad, so she asked her Mom why not.

Her mother told her that her Granddads, like Nanny Rose, had gone to heaven.

Jenny put her hands on her hips and said, 'Oh no! Have we got to mow their lawns as well?'

Liz Milnes

THE TERRIBLE TWOS

My husband and I were having a special blessing service in church. We'd completed the Communion and the Vicar was doing the Ritual Absolution. He lifted the cup drained it, and my young nephew said in a loud whisper, for all to hear, 'Mum, he's drunk the bloody lot'.

Liz Carruthers

I went to Church yesterday, Mothering Sunday, and, as the children were going around giving the Mums small posies of flowers, the Minister stopped one small boy and said:

'Now, where do you go when you want anything, and who do you go to?'

Expecting the small boy to reply, 'Mum', the Minister and the rest of us were shaken when the answer came back, loud and clear, 'Sainsbury's'.

Mary Fawson

My daughter, aged about seven, came home from school and asked, 'What is a prostitute?'

As quick as a flash my youngest daughter, aged about five, replied, 'You know, it's what dad is'.

Shocked silence followed, then I asked her what she meant.

'You know,' she replied, 'not a Catholic.'

Bernadette Gray

My son was always a lively toddler and, in order to keep him quiet during the Sunday service, he was allowed a small toy car which he quietly 'brrr-brrmed' in and around the back pew.

The prayers continued and, at the point when the priest intoned 'Now let us all join together and say the words, "The Lord has taught us ...", his head shot up, the car flew from his hand, and he shouted excitedly, 'What tortoise? Where's the tortoise, Mummy?'

Lesley Polley

THE TERRIBLE TWOS

'MUM, HE'S DRUNK THE BLOODY LOT'.

THE TERRIBLE TWOS

My sister went to a nativity play where the little Virgin Mary became exasperated with the little Lord Jesus and said fiercely: 'Stop your snivelling, Jesus'.

At another nativity, when asked, 'Is there any room at the Inn?' the child replied, 'Oh, yes,' making the story of the stable quite redundant.

Finally, at yet another nativity, in answer to: 'And what shall the child be called?', the reply came back: 'Colin'.

Olive Miles

My father sometimes collected Jo, five years old, from school in the car. On this particular occasion she hadn't eaten all her lunch and was finishing a sandwich. The conversation went like this:

Joanne: 'Daddy, is Jesus everywhere?'

Dad: 'Yes, love, everywhere.'

Joanne: 'Even in this car.'

Dad: 'Yes. He's everywhere.'

Joanne: 'Not in this sandwich?'

Dad (*Emphasizing the point*): 'Yes. He is.'

Joanne (*After long pause*): 'Well, He'd better move over quick then when I take a bite!'

Jaki Russell

Nina was captivated with the story of the nativity, birth and eventual death of Jesus on the cross, and was overjoyed when she was chosen to be an angel in the nativity play. She learnt her lines to perfection.

However, Nina is given to adding her own logic to every situation.

The nativity was well under way and when it was her turn to say her lines to Mary, she said, 'Don't worry, Mary, you will have a lovely baby and you will call him Jesus.'

She then added, 'But I wouldn't get too attached to him, cos he'll be dead by Easter'.

John Marshall

THE TERRIBLE TWOS

Our latest parish magazine revealed the following:
'A young couple and their little daughter were taking an early Spring weekend break in the countryside and, on Sunday morning, went to the nearby village church. The church was minus decoration during Lent, including flowers and organ music.

The four-year-old, puzzled by the unaccustomed silence, asked her mother, 'Why isn't the organ playing, Mummy?'

Heads turned in the congregation to see where the penetrating small voice had come from.

Mother, embarrassed, whispered hastily, 'Because it's Lent, dear,' upon which the same penetrating voice asked, 'Who to?'

Bob

Steven, around six at the time, came home from school and told his Mum and Dad that he was going to be Joseph in the Christmas nativity play, and he had two lines to learn over the weekend.

Come Monday morning, he was word-perfect, and went off to school in a very happy mood.

Alas, when he came home, he was crying, and it emerged that the teacher had told him that he could no longer be Joseph because his little friend was going to be Joseph, and he was going to be the inn keeper instead

From then on, the two little boys were enemies.

Come the evening of the nativity play all was going well — the school hall was packed to capacity, with the local Vicar as guest of honour.

When the part was reached where Mary and Joseph knocked on the inn keeper's door and asked if there was any room at the inn, Steven came from around the scenery and boomed in his loudest voice, 'Yes, Mary can come in, but you can F... off.'

Pauline Sullivan

THE TERRIBLE TWOS

It was Christmas Eve, and my husband was watching the six o'clock news coverage of the riots and demonstrations that were taking place in Bethlehem. The pictures showed great gatherings of people on the streets.

On hearing the name Bethlehem, my son, Andrew, aged seven, looked up from what he was doing:

'Is that Bethlehem, Dad?' he asked.

'Yes,' said my husband.

'What ... Bethlehem where Jesus was born?' Andrew asked.

'Yes,' said my husband.

'Well,' Andrew replied, 'no wonder there was no room for Mary and Joseph at the Inn — there are millions of them.'

Caralyn Mintey

The following took place at the school dinner table where David was the question-master, and Kelly and Amy were the contestants in a quiz game.

David: 'This question is for both of you. The first one to give me the right answer is the winner. Who were the first people on earth?'

Kelly: 'Adam and Eve.'

Amy (*Disgruntled*): It's not fair! I didn't watch that.'

Diane, Ken and Polly Sturgess

A nearby clergyman preaching at the children's anniversary service, was stressing that the Bible is the best book — or the best book is the Bible. He then said to the children, 'Now, remember the three 'Bs' — and if you meet me in the street I want you to be able to tell me that you've remembered my message'.

Lo and behold, a few days later, a little girl, about six years old, ran up to him in the street, saying, 'Oh, Vicar, Vicar, I can remember everything you told us last Sunday about those three WASPS'.

Jean Dawson

THE TERRIBLE TWOS

Many years ago, when my own children were small, there was a bad thunderstorm. The children were standing by the window, watching the rain.

There was an extra loud clap of thunder, and David said:

'I don't like thunder.'

'It won't hurt you,' his sister Maureen replied, 'but I'm afraid it will knock a hole in the sky, and Jesus will fall through.'

Flo Edser

The occasion was a birthday party in the early 1950s, when England was deemed to be a Christian land, and grace was said before meals.

Hence, the Mother of the 'Birthday Boy' was somewhat startled to hear a young guest addressing his devotions to Allah.

At a suitable juncture, she said to the child, 'You seemed to be praying to Allah — surely you meant God?'

'Oh, no,' he replied (expressing himself vehemently with all the scorn that his tender years could muster), 'I've finished with God. I pray to Allah now.'

It then emerged that he had lost his favourite marble and had asked God ever so many times to help him find it, but He didn't.

'I asked Allah only twice,' he added, 'and there it was.'

Mike Trueman

My granddaughter, Stephanie, was taken on an outing to the church nearby.

Being a very chatty little girl, she said to the Vicar, 'My Mummy and Daddy got married here'.

'Yes,' said the Vicar, and then went on to tell the children, 'This is a special place. It's God's house. God is a very special person because He not only sees you all standing here, He can see right inside you.'

'My Daddy is very special, too,' Stephanie chirped up, 'he can see right inside you as well.'

My son is a Consultant Surgeon. *Margaret Fox*

THE TERRIBLE TWOS

"... AND THEN 2000 YEARS AGO, YOU PROBABLY GOT INTO TERRIBLE TROUBLE FROM YOUR MUM FOR WALKING ON THE WATER WITHOUT YOUR WELLIES ...."

THE TERRIBLE TWOS

Teacher to class: 'If Jesus walked into the room at this moment, what would you say to him?'

Little boy instantly : 'I would hand him the Bible and say "This Is Your Life!"

Who could he have been listening to!

Pat Scott

Before my marriage I had attended chapel all my life but, since then, hadn't been near the place. The new Minister must have been gathering in some 'lost sheep' and decided to visit me at home.

My husband who was a policeman at the time, working the late shift, was in the bathroom getting ready for work. As he was in the habit of floating about half-naked when he had finished, I asked my five-year-old daughter to go and warn Daddy that the Minister had come to see me.

She obediently left the room, went to the bottom of the stairs and yelled: 'DADDY ... THE PRIME MINISTER HAS COME TO SEE MUMMY'.

My husband entered the room with a very surprised and enquiring look on his face.

Margaret Lakeman

Before I became a teacher I was a church caretaker. One afternoon, alone in an empty church, I was polishing the floor. I looked up and saw a boy of about four years old gazing at me from the middle of the aisle. There was no one with him and I was about to say hallo, and ask where his mother was, when he turned and ran out.

Alarmed because the church yard led straight on to a busy main road, I ran out after him.

I arrived just in time to hear his mother reprimanding him, saying, 'Don't you ever run away from me again!'

'But, Mummy,' replied the child, 'I only went inside the church to see God, but he wasn't there ... only his wife doing the work.'

Joy Jeffrey

Sex

At the time of the Queen's Jubilee, my two sons were at junior and infant school. The elder one must have thought it was about time his younger brother knew a bit about the facts of life concerning the female body, and had obviously been telling him.

Come the day of the Jubilee, they were having parties at school after which the Headmistress read out a letter from the Queen signed Elizabeth Regina.

When Stewart, the youngest returned from school, I enquired if he had had an enjoyable party?

'Yes,' he replied, 'but hasn't the Queen got a *very rude* name.'

Barbara Rayner

Man was just starting to explore space, and all manned rocket launches were televised to the world.

My son, aged about five or six, and I, were watching one such launch which was getting close to lift-off.

Suddenly, he said, 'Dad, what's sex?'

For a moment, I was flabbergasted. I wasn't expecting such a question so soon. But I thought, 'Lets get it over with and find out what he wants to know. So, I said to him, 'What exactly do you want to know?'

'Well,' he replied, 'it says on the screen four-minutes-ten-secs to lift-off. What's secs?'

Mr G. Bishop

One sunny summer day a group of Mums took their little tots to the beach where they were all playing naked on the sand. The following was overheard:

Little Girl to Little Boy: 'Can I touch it?'

Little Boy to Little Girl: 'No, you've already broken yours off.'

Retired Nanny

THE TERRIBLE TWOS

"— I CAN SEE MY TESTICLES!"

Sitting in my car with my grandson (then three years old),waiting for Mum, he became bored.

Looking into the reverse mirror, he began to pull faces at himself.

Upon opening his mouth wide, he said: 'I can see my testicles'.

You try saying, without falling about laughing, 'No, darling, you mean your tonsils'.

Anne Townsend

THE TERRIBLE TWOS

My son Andrew (now aged thirty-one) was three-years-old at the time this happened.

While being bathed, he looked down at his private bits and said, 'Mummy, is this my brains?'

As you can doubtless imagine Mummy fell about laughing and replied, 'I hope that's not where they are!'

My elder son, Tony, aged about five, came in and said, 'What are you laughing at, Mummy?'

I repeated what Andrew had said and Tony replied, 'Don't be silly, Mummy. He means his veins'.

Ann Whittle

THE TERRIBLE TWOS

Sadly, one of my colleagues was left as a one-parent family with a small boy, Craig, to bring up herself.

From a very early age he was continually asking leading questions, and despite being only twenty-something Mum held strong views that children should be children for as long as possible and was proud of her ability to neatly side-step the questions.

However, as time went by, matters deteriorated, especially when he started playschool.

One day he came home from school, bursting with the news that a classmate had had a new baby sister which had been brought in for inspection.

That night while Mum was bathing him, she decided that, against her better judgement, she had better tell him the Facts of Life.

She wove a story of which she was immensely proud with a central theme of seeds and flowers in the garden, but including Mummies and Daddies and carefully using familiar words when naming the 'parts'. She told him everything: how the baby got in, how it grew and got out, and he sat in the bath absolutely transfixed.

She then lifted him out of the bath, and, while wrapping him in a towel, he asked:

'Mum? D'you have to take your jumper off?'

I understand she explained it was entirely optional!

Jan Owens

When my brother, aged two-and-a-half, was in the bath with me one evening (I was aged four), he suddenly said to our mother — without any just cause or reason:

'If anyone ever asks me to be a Daddy, I shall say NO!'

Sue Reddish

THE TERRIBLE TWOS

This story relates to Charlotte, who is now twenty-one, and a Prime Minister-in-waiting at the London School of Economics.

In 1976, when all the latest and best things were 'digital', Charlotte was taken to visit Father Christmas at the Co-op in Walsall. (By the way, it was September!)

Having been on the mystery sleigh ride, she stood at the old man's knee and pondered what she wanted for Christmas. After thinking long and hard, and going through the usual list of books and games, there was a pause. The cogs churned even harder.

'What I really would like is one of those Genital Watches', she finally said.

Graham Hicken

While staying with my sister, husband and two young sons we decided to visit a garden centre. This was situated in the 'sticks', so we encountered some very uneven roads.

I was sat in the back of the car between the two lads. The youngest, then aged two-and-a-half, urged his dad to go quicker. Wondering what the matter was, I asked why?

'It's great when we go fast,' he said, 'it makes my winkle jump up and down when it's bumpy.'

Claire M. Precious

Many years ago when my nephew was four years old, his father, my brother, used to say to him after he had been to the toilet, 'Put it away, Victor, the ducks will have it.'

Well, they lived in a downstairs flat, and upstairs lived Gladys, aged three. This particular morning she came out on to the balcony with nothing on. Victor looked up, and screamed, 'Dad, Dad, come quick, the ducks have had Gladys's.'

Mrs C. Griffiths

THE TERRIBLE TWOS

Pets

My son, Andrew, was aged about four at the time of this story. We have quite a large garden and he used to love playing out on his pedal car. It was a lovely sunny day and I was doing my housework and checking on him from time to time.

All of a sudden there was an ominous silence.

I checked that the gate had not been opened and then called Andrew's name — nothing. I called again, a bit louder, and heard a muffled 'Mum'.

Following the direction of the sound I went up the garden. We have one of those green compost bins with a flip-top lid. I lifted it to find Andrew flat on his back, arms and legs in the air, and obviously unable to move.

Feeling like Joyce Grenfell, I asked, 'Andrew what are you doing in there?'

'Sam pushed me,' was the reply.

Sam was our cat! *Pam Bellis*

Two close friends have two daughters Nicola (seven years old) and Carina (four years old).

Nicola had been given a hamster for her birthday, and a few weeks later her Mum noticed it wasn't looking too well.

Not wanting to upset Nicola, she took the hamster to the vets, taking Carina with her, while Nicola was at Brownies. Sadly, much to Carina's distress, accompanied by crying and wailing, the vet decided the kindest thing would be to put the hamster to sleep.

Within ten minutes of returning home, typical of children's reactions, Carina was as right as rain.

Mum then fetched Nicola, and decided to wait until they got home before gently telling her the sad news.

As they entered the house, perky-faced Carina rushed up to Nicola, saying excitedly, 'Guess what? Your hamster's DEAD!'

Liz and Tom Newton

THE TERRIBLE TWOS

THE TERRIBLE TWOS

My niece told her son John, who was five years old, that the next day was their dog's birthday and he would be a year old.

'Are you going to make him a cake?' John asked.

His mother explained that dogs don't have birthday cakes, but she would give him some extra dog chocs.

John thought about this for a minute and then said, 'Will lots of other dogs come to tea?'

Elma Cherry

THE TERRIBLE TWOS

Carol and Mom were standing at the bus stop with two small sons.

An elderly lady in the queue admired the two adorable little boys and enquired what they would like to be when they grow up.

Elder boy: 'I want to be a fireman.'

Younger boy: 'I want to be an Alsatian.'

M. Gauntlett

I was trying to warn my son, Fergus, aged two-and-a-half, that not all dogs are as friendly as our own dog, Luke (a Springer Spaniel, with a heart of gold, who had been suffering silently while small hands, large toys, etc., were being stuffed into his mouth, and was still managing to smile weakly).

As I went on, I could tell that I was getting more and more bogged down in my explanation, and, not wanting to confuse Fergus by telling him that Luke is a gun dog with a very soft mouth, I told him that Luke could carry birds and small animals, like rabbits, in his mouth without hurting them, whereas other dogs would probably bite them.

Fergus thought for a while, then said: 'Luke can carry little animals in his mouth, Mummy.'

Me: 'Yes.'

Fergus: 'He wouldn't carry a giraffe, would he?'

The vision of the dog with a giraffe between his teeth was too much, and at that point I gave up!

Gabrielle Ewbank

Motorists

My daughter, aged four, was in the car, being driven to Sunday School when, suddenly, another car driver very foolishly pulled out in front of us.

'Stupid prick,' my daughter yelled out of the open window, just as we arrived at the church door for all to hear.

Janis Cunningham

Overheard in a car park yesterday.

Little girl to her Mother (who was driving):

'Mummy, on the way home, I want you to sit in the back with me.'

Joan Ray

THE TERRIBLE TWOS

"STUPID PRICK!"

Grandmas and Grandpas

While sitting in front of the mirror doing my make-up, my granddaughter, Hayley, asked:

'Why do you put that stuff on your face?'

'To make me look beautiful,' I replied.

'When will it start to work?' she asked.

Lorna Compton

My four-year-old granddaughter, Katherine, was lying on the carpet next to me as I got on with the ironing.

I became aware that she had turned over on to her back and was looking up my skirt.

'Katherine,' I said crossly, 'what are you doing?'

'Grandma,' she replied indignantly, 'I am trying to see if you have Mickey Mouse on your knickers.'

Nancy Neocleous

This would amuse Desmond Morris.

Our granddaughter, aged about four, was standing by my husband's chair. Suddenly, she picked up his hand and said,

'Is this your last skin, Grandpa?'

Kathleen Mason

We have four grandchildren, the youngest Gavin being three years old and going through the finicky food syndrome.

Trying to persuade him to eat his lunch, I said he wouldn't grow curly hair if he didn't eat his veg.

'I'm a little boy,' he replied, 'I'm not a girl. I don't need curly hair.'

Not to be outdone, I said, 'Well, your Daddy's got really lovely curly hair'.

'Yes,' he replied, 'that's cos he ate too many vegetables when he was a little boy.'

Trixie Taylor

THE TERRIBLE TWOS

THE TERRIBLE TWOS

I am a fairly fit fifty-four year old, and need to be as my grandchildren Carl and Amy are nearly four and two-and-a-half.

At Christmas, a very ancient crib scene comes out complete with Mary, Joseph, kings, shepherds and baby Jesus, all made by my sons Blue Peter-fashion out of loo rolls, etc.

Amy especially loved baby Jesus and each time she went into the lounge she picked Him up, gave Him a kiss, and put Him back into the manger.

After Christmas she went into the lounge and stopped dead, 'Oh,' she said, 'baby Jesus gone!'

I explained that, now that Christmas was over, I had packed everything carefully away.

'Where?' asked Amy.

'In the loft ready for next year,' I answered.

'Oh, right,' she said, trotting away.

While this conversation was going on Carl was looking at several photos, grouped together in a large frame.

'Who's that, Nan?' he asked.

I told him and so it continued right through all the photos, until he came to one of my husband:

'And who's that, Nan?'

'That's Granddad Irvine, darling,' I replied.

'Where is he, Nan?'

'He died when you were a baby.'

'Where is he now, Nan?'

'He has gone to heaven to live with Jesus.'

He paused, then added:

'Is he in the loft, Nan?'

I know I put a great many things in the loft, but ...!

Patricia Irvine

THE TERRIBLE TWOS

My grandson Michael is now ten, but, when he first started school, Mummy asked him on his return home what he had had for school dinner.

'Wind in the Willow Hole,' he replied.

After a few more questions, it turned out that he had had 'Toad in the Hole'.

Well, he was almost right!

Doreen Ralph

When putting flowers on Grandma's grave, my young son asked,

'Do you fink she can see the flowers?'

'I shouldn't really think so,' I said.

'Perhaps, she can just see the stalks,' he replied.

Audrey of Beccles

We took our four-year-old grandson, Joseph, to the 'Teddy Bears' Concert' at the Barbican.

He enjoyed the afternoon, joining in the sing-a-longs, and, at various times, went to the loo with either me or grandpa.

On return home, his Mummy asked:

'What was the best part of the concert, Joseph?'

Without a moment's hesitation, he replied:

'Going to the toilet with Grandpa.'

Rosalind Harris

THE TERRIBLE TWOS

I had a visit from my three granddaughters, Rebecca, three, and five-year-old twins Bethan and Cara.

Chatting, as you do about life, the twins began discussing what they'd do when they grew up.

'Who would you like to marry?' I asked.

'John in my class in school,' Bethan replied.

'What about you, Cara?' I said.

'I don't know,' she replied.

'What boy do you like best in your class?' I asked helpfully.

'Mark,' she said.

'There you are,' I replied, 'you can marry him.'

'I can't.' Cara said. 'He's already got a sister.'

Dorothy Mead

My grandson, Matthew, at about two-and-a-half years old, was playing happily in the garden in his sandpit. Mummy was upstairs making the beds.

'Mummy,' Matthew called up. 'It's cold outside, can I come and play indoors?'

'Of course you can, darling,' Mummy said. 'I will be down soon and we will have lunch.'

Some time later Mummy came downstairs, and put her head round the lounge door. There, in the middle of her BRAND NEW carpet, was Matthew playing with his sandpit!

He had filled his toy wheelbarrow with sand, obviously making several trips to and from the garden, and was quite happily making sandpies, etc.

'Hallo, Mummy,' he smiled sweetly!

Doreen Wilkinson

THE TERRIBLE TWOS

I had my two grandchildren staying with me, and having put them to bed, I staggered down stairs to put my feet up.

A few minutes later, I heard Sarah crying, and went up to ask her what was the matter.

'I am frightened, Granny,' she said.

When I asked why, my grandson said:

'I'm not frightened of anything, Granny.'

Then, after a long pause, he continued:

'Except for the dinosaurs and witches that came through your window.'

You can imagine the effect this had on Sarah!

Betty Atkins

THE TERRIBLE TWOS

My grandson Luke, aged five, was sitting in the kitchen one day playing with my lettuce-spinner.

'Don't break it, dear,' I said, 'I often use it to spin my pants in ...'

At which, as he took one look at the size of my bottom, we both roared with laughter.

But when I went to his 'open day' at school and read his 'newsletter', the laugh, I'm afraid, was on me.

He had written, 'my grandma spins her pants in the lettuce spinner. I don't know how she gets them in, they're such a size ...'

Nice, eh. Who wants grandchildren?

Ruth Watson

At my age, my hair is a mixture of white, black and grey. One day my granddaughter looked up into my face and said, 'I don't know what colour your hair is, Nana, but I don't like it.'

Beryl Gawthorne

THE TERRIBLE TWOS

Granddad spent absolutely ages fitting some stabilizers to our granddaughter Katy's first two-wheeler.

She jumped on the bike — pedalled once up and down the cul-de-sac came back, and said, 'Right, Granddad, I've got the hang of it. You can take them off again'.

Irene Cain

Some years ago, when my grandchildren were over here from America, I took them to see the plaque placed near to Deal Castle recording the landing on the nearby beach of Julius Caesar in the year 55 BC.

My grandson — then aged about four-and-a-half — turned to me and said, 'Were you living here then, Nanna?'

Esme Mackins

ACKNOWLEDGEMENTS

Special thanks are due to the following people who have freely and very generously donated contributions to this book to support BBC Children in Need:

Contributors to
Sarah Kennedy's BBC Radio Two programme
who have given permission for their
letters to be included in this book.

Cartoonists

Barry Appleby
Neil Bennett
Simon Bond
Chris Burke
Clive Collins
Frank Dickens
Maurice Dodd
Dorrien
Hunt Emerson
Haro
Jim Hutchings
Kathryn Lamb
Larry
Mac
Sue Macartney-Snape
Peter Maddocks
Matt
Bill Mevin
Geo Parkin
Ken Pyne
Posy Simmonds
Trog

Paul Gravett
The National Museum of Cartoon Art
'Carriage Row,'
183 Eversholt Street,
London NW1 1DD